for

_____

and

_____

with Best Wishes on Your

Wedding
Anniversary

from

_____

_____*19*_____

For my parents,
Mr. & Mrs. L. J. Caldwell,
whose love through the years has been
one of my richest treasures.

THROUGH THE YEARS

An Anniversary Remembrance

Louis O. Caldwell

Drawings by Harriette Bateman

ABINGDON PRESS
Nashville and New York

Through the Years

Copyright © 1975 by Abingdon Press

Library of Congress Cataloging in Publication Data

Caldwell, Louis O.
   Through the years.
   1. Marriage—Quotations, maxims, etc. I. Title.
PN6084.M3C3   808.88'2   74-34374
        ISBN 0-687-42059-8

Acknowledgment is made to the owners and copyright holders for
permission to reprint the following materials:
   "Service to Celebrate a Silver or Golden Wedding Anniversary,"
from *The Cokesbury Marriage Manual* by William Leach, copyright
renewal 1973 by Ethel K. Leach, used by permission of Abingdon
Press. Excerpts from *We Can Have Better Marriages* by David and
Vera Mace, copyright © 1974 by Abingdon Press.
   "The Power of Love," reprinted from *America*, © 1964 by
America Press.
   Selections by Louis O. Caldwell from *Meditations for Modern
Marrieds*, copyright © 1974 by Baker Book House, and *The Adven-
ture of Becoming One*, copyright © 1969 by Baker Book House.
   Selections from the Jerusalem Bible, copyright © 1966 by Dar-
ton, Longman & Todd, Ltd., and Doubleday & Company, Inc.

Manufactured by the Parthenon Press at
Nashville, Tennessee, United States of America

Preface

"What's so remarkable about love at first sight?" asks an unknown writer; adding, "It's when people have been looking at each other for years that it becomes remarkable." And when couples manage to achieve this kind of love relationship, a celebration is in order! Perhaps the wedding anniversary could be defined as an annual celebration not just of the marriage ceremony, but more important, of the triumph of their love.

To contribute to the celebration of your wedding anniversary is the purpose of this book. Its design and contents were chosen so as to invest your anniversary with its deepest possible meaning.

These timeless tributes to love and marriage not only enable husband and wife to *celebrate* an anniversary, but also to acknowledge the ever present help of their great unseen Guest. For we remember that Christ performed his first miracle for a young couple starting life together. And there can be no doubt that if his presence brought joy at the beginning of the journey, how much greater the joy for those continuing on their way.

Louis O. Caldwell

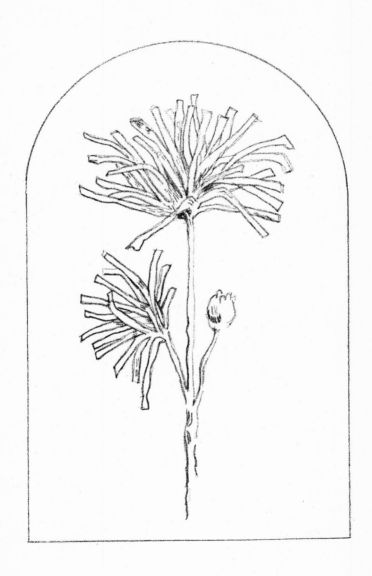

Time
is
Too slow for those who wait,
Too swift for those who fear,
Too long for those who grieve,
Too short for those who rejoice,
But for those who love, time is
Eternity.
Hours fly,
Flowers die,
New days,
New ways,
Pass by.
Love stays.

—Inscription on a sundial
University of Virginia

His banner over me was love.

—Song of Solomon 2:4

His left hand is under my head, and his right hand doth embrace me.

—Song of Solomon 2:6

All paths lead to you
  Where e'er I stray,
You are the evening star
  At the end of day.

All paths lead to you
  Hill-top or low,
You are the white birch
  In the sun's glow.

All paths lead to you
  Where e'er I roam.
You are the lark-song
  Calling me home!

—*Blanche Shoemaker Wagstaff*

My beloved spake, and said unto me, Rise up, my love, my fair one, and come away. For, lo, the winter is past, the rain is over and gone; the flowers appear on the earth; the time of the singing of birds is come, and the voice of the turtle is heard in our land; the fig tree putteth forth her green figs, and the vines with the tender grape give a good smell. Arise, my love, my fair one, and come away.

—*Song of Solomon 2:10-13*

My beloved is mine, and I am his.

—*Song of Solomon 2:16*

Many husbands and wives, I believe, make the mistake of expecting too much early in marriage, and then of expecting too little later on.

—*David R. Mace*

Since the greatest of all the arts is the art of living together and since the highest and most permanent happiness depends on it, and since the way to practice this art successfully lies through character, the supreme question is how to obtain character.

The surest way is through religion—religion in the home. All that we know for certain of every person is that he is imperfect. Human imperfection means a chronic need for improvement. The most tremendous and continuous elevating, purifying, strengthening force is religious faith.

—*William Lyon Phelps*

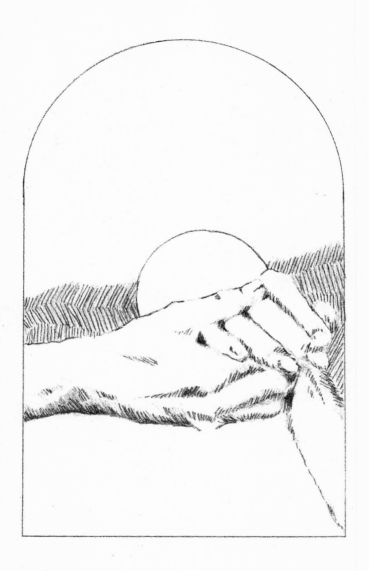

To earn the respect, trust, and love of our mate and children is the most noble achievement of adulthood. Such an achievement reflects the wisdom of setting proper priorities and the development of the finest qualities of personhood.

Writing in this vein, Joseph Parker, one of the greatest preachers of the nineteenth century, noted, "The practical question is, 'How do we mean to be known?' . . . There is a fame of the heart, a fame of goodness, a fame of charity; there is a household glory. A man may be famous at home. The day has not begun until he comes in; the home is only a house until she who is loved appears upon the scene; the house is only furnished by the cabinet-maker, not lighted up by the genius of home, until such and such a life is realised in its holy and happy presence. . . . To be famous under his own roof, should be the ambition of every man. . . . We should covet the fame of love, the fame of household trust, the fame of the heart."

We have lived and loved together
  Through many changing years;
We have shared each other's gladness
  And wept each other's tears;
I have known ne'er a sorrow
  That was long unsoothed by thee;
For thy smiles can make a summer
  Where darkness else would be.

Like the leaves that fall around us
  In autumn's fading hours,
Are the traitor's smiles, that darken
  When the cloud of sorrow lowers;
And though many such we've known, love,
  Too prone, alas, to range,
We both can speak of one love
  Which time can never change.

We have lived and loved together
  Through many changing years,
We have shared each other's gladness
  And wept each other's tears.
And let us hope the future,
  As the past has been will be:
I will share with thee my sorrows,
  And thou thy joys with me.

—Charles Jefferys

This, then, is what I pray, kneeling before the Father, from whom every family, whether spiritual or natural, takes its name:

> Out of his infinite glory, may he give you the power through his Spirit for your hidden self to grow strong, so that Christ may live in your hearts through faith, and then, planted in love and built on love, you will with all the saints have strength to grasp the breadth and the length, the height and the depth; until, knowing the love of Christ, which is beyond all knowledge, you are filled with the utter fulness of God.

—Ephesians 3:14-19
The Jerusalem Bible

Yet I would not have all yet.
He that hath all can have no more;
And since my love doth every day admit
New growth, thou shouldst have new rewards in store;
Thou canst not every day give me thy heart.
If thou canst give it, then thou never gavest it;
Love's riddles are, that though thy heart depart,
It stays at home, and thou with losing savest it:
But we will have a way more liberal
Than changing hearts, to join them; so we shall
  Be one, and one another's all.

—John Donne

The fountains mingle with the river
And the rivers with the Ocean,
The winds of Heaven mix for ever
With a sweet emotion;
Nothing in the world is single;
All things by a law divine
In one spirit meet and mingle
Why not I with thine?—

See the mountains kiss high Heaven
And the waves clasp one another;
No sister-flower would be forgiven
If it disdained its brother;
And the sunlight clasps the earth
And the moonbeams kiss the sea:
What is all this sweet work worth
If thou kiss not me?

—Percy Bysshe Shelley

A survey of modern marital trends gives substance to the doubts expressed by a growing number of people who are disturbed over the temporary nature of many marriage commitments. In his book *Hans Frost*, Hugh Walpole has Nathalie asking Uncle Hans, "Does love never last?"

Uncle Hans' reply is worth deep consideration: "Love can last if you get two people who are fine enough. But they must both be fine, and trouble is that the right people so seldom meet. You see it sometimes. A man has had the luck to encounter a woman who compels all the grand things in him—unselfishness, honor, gaiety, gladness. . . . But for the most part people aren't patient enough, and they blame others for their own failings."

In this connection André Maurois has expressed deep wisdom: "I have chosen; from now on my aim will be, not to search for someone who may please me, but to please the one I have chosen."

—*Louis O. Caldwell*

O my luve is like a red, red rose,
That's newly sprung in June:
O my luve is like the melodie,
That's sweetly play'd in tune.

As fair art thou, my bonie lass,
So deep in luve am I;
And I will luve thee still, my dear,
Till a' the seas gang dry.

Till a' the seas gang dry, my dear,
And the rocks melt wi' the sun;
And I will luve thee still, my dear,
While the sands o' life shall run.

And fare thee weel, my only luve!
And fare thee weel a while!
And I will come again, my luve,
Tho' it were ten thousand mile.

—Robert Burns

Though I speak with the tongues of men and of angels, and have not charity, I am become as sounding brass, or a tinkling cymbal.

And though I have the gift of prophecy, and understand all mysteries, and all knowledge; and though I have all faith, so that I could remove mountains, and have not charity, I am nothing.

And though I bestow all my goods to feed the poor, and though I give my body to be burned, and have not charity, it profiteth me nothing.

Charity suffereth long, and is kind; charity envieth not; charity vaunteth not itself, is not puffed up,

Doth not behave itself unseemly, seeketh not her own, is not easily provoked, thinketh no evil;

Rejoiceth not in iniquity, but rejoiceth in the truth;

Beareth all things, believeth all things, hopeth all things, endureth all things.

Charity never faileth: but whether there be prophecies, they shall fail; whether there be tongues, they shall cease; whether there be knowledge, it shall vanish away.

For we know in part, and we prophesy in part.

But when that which is perfect is come, then that which is in part shall be done away.

When I was a child, I spake as a child, I understood as a child, I thought as a child: but when I became a man, I put away childish things.

For now we see through a glass, darkly; but then face to face: now I know in part; but then shall I know even as also I am known.

And now abideth faith, hope, charity, these three; but the greatest of these is charity.

—I Corinthians 13

Set me as a seal upon thine heart, as a seal upon thine arm: for love is strong as death.

—Song of Solomon 8:6

And Ruth said, Entreat me not to leave thee, or to return from following after thee: for whither thou goest, I will go; and where thou lodgest, I will lodge: thy people shall be my people, and thy God my God: where thou diest, will I die, and there will I be buried: the Lord do so to me, and more also, if aught but death part thee and me.

—Ruth 1:16-17

I love you
Not only for what you are,
But for what I am
When I am with you.

I love you,
Not only for what
You have made of yourself,
But for what
You are making of me.

I love you
For the part of me
That you bring out;
I love you
For putting your hand
Into my heaped-up heart
And passing over
All foolish, weak things
That you can't help
Dimly seeing there,
And for drawing out
Into the light
All the beautiful belongings
That no one else had looked
Quite far enough to find.

I love you because you
Are helping me to make
Of the lumber of my life
Not a tavern
But a temple;
Out of the works
Of my every day
Not a reproach
But a song.

—*Roy Croft*

Many waters cannot quench love, neither can the floods drown it: if a man would give all the substance of his house for love, it would utterly be contemned.

—*Song of Solomon 8:7*

My vineyard, which is mine, is before me.

—*Song of Solomon 8:12*

Thou that dwellest in the gardens, the companions hearken to thy voice: cause me to hear it.

—*Song of Solomon 8:13*

Make haste, my beloved, and be thou like to a roe or to a young hart upon the mountains of spices.

—*Song of Solomon 8:14*

As unto the bow the cord is,
So unto the man is woman,
Though she bends him, she obeys him,
Though she draws him, yet she follows,
Useless each without the other!

—*Henry Wadsworth Longfellow*

Two lovers by a moss-grown spring:
They leaned soft cheeks together there,
Mingled the dark and sunny hair,
And heard the wooing thrushes sing.
> O budding time!
> O love's blest prime!

Two wedded from the portal stept:
The bells made happy carollings,
The air was soft as fanning wings,
White petals on the pathway slept.
> O pure-eyed bride!
> O tender pride!

Two faces o'er a cradle bent:
Two hands above the head were locked:
These pressed each other while they rocked,
Those watched a life that love had sent.
> O solemn hour!
> O hidden power!

Two parents by the evening fire:
The red light fell about their knees
On heads that rose by slow degrees
Like buds upon the lily spire.
> O patient life!
> O tender strife!

The two still sat together there,
The red light shone about their knees;
But all the heads by slow degrees
Had gone and left that lonely pair.
> O voyage fast!
> O vanished past!

The red light shone upon the floor
And made the space between them wide;
They drew their chairs up side by side,
Their pale cheeks joined, and said, "Once more!"
   O memories!
   O past that is!

—George Eliot

Live joyfully with the wife whom thou lovest all the days of the life of thy vanity, which he hath given thee under the sun, all the days of thy vanity: for that is thy portion in this life, and in thy labor which thou takest under the sun.

—Ecclesiastes 9:9

Jenny kissed me when we met,
Jumping from the chair she sat in;
Time, you thief, who love to get
Sweets into your list, put that in:
Say I'm weary, say I'm sad,
Say that health and wealth have missed me,
Say I'm growing old, but add,
Jenny kissed me.

—Leigh Hunt

Let us be guests in one another's house
With deferential "No" and courteous "Yes";
Let us take care to hide our foolish moods
Behind a certain show of cheerfulness.

Let us avoid all sullen silences;
We should find fresh and sprightly things to say;
I must be fearful lest you find me dull,
And you must dread to bore me any way.

Let us knock gently at each other's heart,
Glad of a chance to look within—and yet
Let us remember that to force one's way
Is the unpardoned breach of etiquette.

So shall I be hostess—you, the host—
Until all need for entertainment ends;
We shall be lovers when the last door shuts,
But what is better still—we shall be friends.

—Carol Haynes

Marriage is more than your love for each other. It has a higher dignity and power, for it is God's holy ordinance, through which he wills to perpetuate the human race till the end of time. In your love you see only your two selves in the world, but in marriage you are a link in the chain of the generations, which God causes to come and to pass away to his glory, and calls into his kingdom. In your love you see only the heaven of your happiness, but in marriage you are placed at a post of responsibility towards the world and mankind. Your love is your own private possession, but marriage is more than something personal—it is a status, an office.

—*Dietrich Bonhoeffer*

Just as it is the crown, and not merely the will to rule, that makes the king, so it is marriage, and not merely your love for each other, that joins you together in the sight of God and man. As high as God is above man, so high are the sanctity, the rights, and the promise of marriage above the sanctity, the rights, and the promise of love. It is not your love that sustains marriage, but from now on, the marriage that sustains your love.

—*Dietrich Bonhoeffer*

Believe me, if all those endearing young charms,
  Which I gaze on so fondly to-day,
Were to change by to-morrow, and fleet in my arms,
  Like fairy-gifts fading away,
Thou wouldst still be adored, as this moment thou art,
  Let thy loveliness fade as it will,
And around the dear ruin each wish of my heart
  Would entwine itself verdantly still.

It is not while beauty and youth are thine own,
  And thy cheeks unprofaned by a tear,
That the fervor and faith of a soul may be known,
  To which time will but make thee more dear;
No, the heart that has truly loved never forgets,
  But as truly loves on to the close,
As the sun-flower turns on her god, when he sets,
  The same look which she turned when he rose.

—*Thomas Moore*

Much has been written about love. But most of the writing, as Pierre Teilhard de Chardin has remarked, concerns "only the sentimental face of love, the joy and miseries it causes us." Relatively little has been set down about love as a way of life. And the power of love, which is the power of Being itself, has been all but passed over. . . .

The reason why an encounter with love moves us so deeply is that, no matter how humble and fleeting the gesture that embodies it, it dramatically recalls to us our own vocations as persons. For the person is not a mere element caught up in nature's restless process. . . . In the person, the transcendent power and creative freedom of God Himself are unleashed in their own right. To be a person is to share in Being itself and in Being's creative concern for all that is. . . . The person who lives as a person . . . is one who has learned that to be is to love, to spend oneself for others that they may more truly be, and that in the spending one is not impoverished but evermore deeply rooted in that limitless abundance on which one draws.

This is the secret of love's power over us. To be loved is to encounter Being itself, eternity in time, God's face among the faces of men. The loving person translates for our benefit the exuberant life of God in human terms. . . . In the one who loves us we hear God's voice in the realm of everyday. . . . The only thing is not to let it go unanswered.

—*Robert O. Johann*
"The Power of Love "

When, in disgrace with fortune and men's eyes,
I all alone beweep my outcast state,
And trouble deaf heaven with my bootless cries,
And look upon myself, and curse my fate,
Wishing me like to one more rich in hope,
Featur'd like him, like him with friends possess'd,
Desiring this man's art, and that man's scope,
With what I most enjoy contented least;
Yet in these thoughts myself almost despising,
Haply I think on thee,—and then my state,
Like to the lark at break of day arising
From sullen earth, sings hymns, at heaven's gate;
   For thy sweet love remember'd, such wealth brings
   That then I scorn to change my state with kings.

—William Shakespeare

How do I love thee? Let me count the ways.
I love thee to the depth and breadth and height
My soul can reach, when feeling out of sight
For the ends of Being and ideal Grace.
I love thee to the level of every day's
Most quiet need, by sun and candlelight.
I love thee freely, as men strive for Right;
I love thee purely, as they turn from Praise.
I love thee with the passion put to use
In my old griefs, and with my childhood's faith.
I love thee with a love I seemed to lose
With my lost saints,—I love thee with the breath,
Smiles, tears, of all my life!—and, if God choose,
I shall but love thee better after death.

—*Elizabeth Barrett Browning*

To every thing there is a season, and a time to every purpose under the heaven.

—*Ecclesiastes 3:1*

A time to cast away stones, and a time to gather stones together; a time to embrace, and a time to refrain from embracing.

—*Ecclesiastes 3:5*

A time to get, and a time to lose; a time to keep, and a time to cast away.

—*Ecclesiastes 3:6*

Becoming one, in the finest sense, involves sharing more than joys and sorrows. According to the sociologist J. D. Unwin, a marriage can never fully mature unless the partners share an allegiance to some purpose outside themselves which they consider to be ultimately more important than themselves or their relationships.

Actually, mature love is a great alchemy created by goals and purposes that are mutually attractive. This concept is not as generally understood as it needs to be. As Antoine de Saint-Exupery said, "True love does not consist in gazing at each other, but looking outward together in the same direction."

This focuses attention on the crux of the matter. Becoming increasingly one on the human level is a potential relationship that can be actualized only as each partner grows in conformity to the image of Christ. The problem must go beyond finding something to live for, to finding someone to live for. The great principle underlying the deepest kind of merging of husband and wife has not to do with mere physical relations, things, circumstances, philosophy or vague mysticism. Only mutual commitment to Christ enables human beings to transcend their weaknesses and grow increasingly in oneness. The exalting result is that as they get closer and closer to Christ they get closer and closer to each other. The great principle then is this: It takes three to make one—you, your mate and the living Christ.

—*Louis O. Caldwell*

Let all thy joys be as the month of May,
And all thy days be as a marriage day.

—*Francis Quarles*

Once the realization is accepted that even between the *closest* human beings infinite distances continue to exist, wonderful living side by side can grow up, if they succeed in loving the distance between them which makes it possible for each to see the other whole against the sky.

—*Rainer Maria Rilke*

I would ask of you, my darling,
  A question soft and low,
That gives me many a heartache
  As the moments come and go.

Your love I know is truthful,
  But the truest love grows cold;
It is this that I would ask you:
  Will you love me when I'm old?

  Life's morn will soon be waning,
    And its evening bells be tolled,
  But my heart shall know no sadness,
    If you'll love me when I'm old.

Down the stream of life together
  We are sailing side by side,
Hoping some bright day to anchor
  Safe beyond the surging tide.
Today our sky is cloudless,
  But the night may clouds unfold;
But, though storms may gather round us,
  Will you love me when I'm old?

When my hair shall shade the snowdrift,
  And mine eyes shall dimmer grow,
I would lean upon some loved one,
  Through the valley as I go.
I would claim of you a promise,
  Worth to me a world of gold;
It is only this, my darling,
  That you'll love me when I'm old.

—Unknown

Married living needs the continuance of the dash and sparkle of romantic love. But the relation of romantic love to married love is somewhat like that of a little tree to the larger tree which it later becomes. It has life and fresh young energy that enables it to grow. When it has grown into a larger tree its heart and vitality are still there but, with continued life, it has taken new rings of growth, its branches have spread wider and its roots have gone deeper. Moreover it bears flowers and fruit which the little tree did not produce.

Married love is love woven into a pattern of living. It has in it the elements of understanding and of the passionate kindness of husband and wife toward each other. It is rich in the many-sided joys of life because each is more concerned with giving joy than with grasping it for himself. And joys are most truly experienced when they are most fully shared.

—*Leland Foster Wood*

If ever two were one, then surely we.
If ever man were lov'd by wife, then thee.
If ever wife was happy in a man,
Compare with me, ye women, if you can.
I prize thy love more than whole mines of gold,
Of all the riches that the East doth hold.
My love is such that rivers cannot quench,
Nor ought but love from thee give recompense.
Thy love is such I can no way repay;
The heavens reward thee manifold I pray.
Then while we live, in love let's so persevere,
That when we live no more, we may live ever.

—Anne Bradstreet

I have remembered beauty in the night,
  Against black silences I waked to see
  A shower of sunlight over Italy
And green Ravello dreaming on her height;
I have remembered music in the dark,
  The clean swift brightness of a fugue of Bach's,
  And running water singing on the rocks
When once in English woods I heard a lark.

But all remembered beauty is no more
  Than a vague prelude to the thought of you—
  You are the rarest soul I ever knew,
    Lover of beauty, knightliest and best;
My thoughts seek you as waves that seek the shore,
    And when I think of you, I am at rest.

—Sara Teasdale

The kindest and the happiest pair
Will find occasion to forbear,
And something every day they live
To pity, and perhaps forgive.

—William Cowper

How beautiful is the marriage of two Christians, two who are one in hope, one in desire, one in the way of life they follow, one in the religion they practise. . . . Nothing divides them, either in flesh or in spirit. They pray together, they worship together, they fast together; instructing one another. Side by side they visit God's Church and partake of God's banquet; side by side they face difficulties and persecution, share their consolations. They have no secrets from one another; they never shun each other's company; they never bring sorrow to each other's hearts. They visit the sick and assist the needy. . . . Psalms and hymns they sing to one another, striving to see which of them will chant more beautifully the praises of their Lord. Hearing and seeing this, Christ rejoices. To such as these He gives His peace. Where there are two together, there also He is present.

—Tertullian
Treatises on Marriage and Remarriage

Let me not to the marriage of true minds
Admit impediments. Love is not love
Which alters when it alteration finds,
Or bends with the remover to remove:
O, no! it is an ever-fixed mark,
That looks on tempests and is never shaken;
It is the star to every wandering bark,
Whose worth's unknown, although his height be
*   taken.*
Love's not Time's fool, though rosy lips and cheeks
Within his bending sickle's compass come;
Lover alters not with his brief hours and weeks,
But bears it out even to the edge of doom.
*   If this be error, and upon me prov'd,*
*   I never writ, nor no man ever lov'd.*

—William Shakespeare

Marriage has too often been portrayed as two people frozen together side by side, as immobile as marble statues. More accurately, it is the intricate and graceful cooperation of two dancers who through long practice have learned to match each other's movements and moods in response to the music of the spheres.

—David and Vera Mace

There is no more lovely, friendly and charming relationship, communion or company than a good marriage.

—*Martin Luther*

If you should go before me, dear, walk slowly
Down the ways of death, well-worn and wide,
For I would want to overtake you quickly
And seek the journey's ending by your side.

I would be so forlorn not to descry you
Down some shining highroad when I came;
Walk slowly, dear, and often look behind you
And pause to hear if someone calls your name.

—*Adelaide Love*

The heart that loves is always young.

—*Greek Proverb*

How shall I hold my soul, that it may not
be touching yours? How shall I lift it then
above you to where other things are waiting?
Ah, gladly would I lodge it, all-forgot,
with some lost thing the dark is isolating
on some remote and silent spot that, when
your depths vibrate, is not itself vibrating.
You and me—all that lights upon us, though,
brings us together like a fiddle-bow
drawing one voice from two strings it glides along.
Across what instrument have we been spanned?
And what violinist holds us in his hand?
O sweetest song.

—Rainer Maria Rilke

He who loves is a slave; he who is loved is a master.

—Polish Proverb

Marriage is a seam of dreams.

—Frank Crane

Marriage that is truly Christian walks the Emmaus road. The wondrous effect of the marriage journey with Christ as our companion was expressed in 1669 by Thomas and Mary Ellwood, a Quaker couple: "We sensibly felt the Lord with us and joining us, the sense whereof remained with us all our lifetime, and was of very good service and very comfortable to us on all occasions."

Whoever lives true life will love true life.

—*Elizabeth Barrett Browning*

A man is not where he lives, but where he loves.

—*Latin Proverb*

Who can find a virtuous woman? for her price is far above rubies.

The heart of her husband doth safely trust in her, so that he shall have no need of spoil.

She will do him good and not evil all the days of her life.

She seeketh wool, and flax, and worketh willingly with her hands.

She is like the merchants' ships; she bringeth her food from afar.

She riseth also while it is yet night, and giveth meat to her household, and a portion to her maidens.

She considereth a field, and buyeth it: with the fruit of her hands she planteth a vineyard.

She girdeth her loins with strength, and strengtheneth her arms.

She perceiveth that her merchandise is good: her candle goeth not out by night.

She layeth her hands to the spindle, and her hands hold the distaff.

She stretcheth out her hand to the poor; yea, she reacheth forth her hands to the needy.

She is not afraid of the snow for her household: for all her household are clothed with scarlet.

She maketh herself coverings of tapestry; her clothing is silk and purple.

Her husband is known in the gates, when he sitteth among the elders of the land.

She maketh fine linen, and selleth it; and delivereth girdles unto the merchant.

Strength and honor are her clothing; and she shall rejoice in time to come.

She openeth her mouth with wisdom; and in her tongue is the law of kindness.

She looketh well to the ways of her household, and eateth not the bread of idleness.

Her children arise up, and call her blessed; her husband also, and he praiseth her.

Many daughters have done virtuously, but thou excellest them all.

Favor is deceitful, and beauty is vain: but a woman that feareth the Lord, she shall be praised.

Give her of the fruit of her hands; and let her own works praise her in the gates.

—Proverbs 31:10-31

This is the true measure of love, when we believe that we alone can love, that no one could ever have loved so before us, and that no one will ever love in the same way after us.

—Johann Wolfgang von Goethe

To love means to decide independently to live with an equal partner, and to subordinate oneself to the formation of a new subject, a "we."

—Fritz Kunkel

Let there be spaces in your togetherness.
—Kahlil Gibran

It is the man and woman united that makes the complete human being. Separate she lacks his force of body and strength of reason; he her softness, sensibility and acute discernment. Together they are most likely to succeed in the world.

—Benjamin Franklin

It is difficult to define love. But we may say that in the soul, it is a ruling passion; in the mind, it is a close sympathy and affinity; in the body, a wholly secret and delicate longing to possess what we love—and this after much mystery.

—La Rochefoucauld

Jacob served seven years for Rachel; and they seemed unto him but a few days, for the love he had to her.

—*Genesis 29:20*

This is my beloved, and this is my friend.

—*Song of Solomon 5:16*

And this I pray, that your love may abound yet more and more in knowledge and in all judgment.

—*Philippians 1:9*

Beloved, let us love one another: for love is of God; and every one that loveth is born of God, and knoweth God.

—*I John 4:7*

An Anniversary Prayer

Our Heavenly Father,

On this day made so meaningful by what we commemorate together as husband and wife, we express our gratitude to you for your providential care.

Give us the wisdom to use our past in ways that enrich our present and empower us to give expression to the understanding that we now have.

Sharpen our perception of the future as promised in the Scriptures to all believers, that we will be future-oriented, and thus continue to dream youthfully.

Allow us to enter ever more deeply into the mystery of our relationship with each other and with you.

And with each passing day may our union realize its highest purpose, that Christ be glorified by the quality of our lives now mystically merged into one flesh.

This we reverently ask in Christ's name.
Amen.

A Suggestion for Celebrating Your Marriage Anniversary*

Special occasions are only as important as the meaning they have for the participants. John Steinbeck in his novel *Burning Bright,* has Joe Saul express an insight that suggests the means by which we can deepen the meaning of the wedding anniversary. Upon hearing from his wife that they are expecting a child, Saul, ecstatic with joy, confides to a close friend: "I want to bring a present to her . . . something like a ceremony, something like a golden sacrament, some pearl like a prayer or a red flaming ruby of thanks. . . . I must get this thing. My joy requires a symbol."

Like Saul, we feel a need for a symbol, but one that is appropriate for celebrating the marriage anniversary. The kind of symbol I would like to recommend is a cup, either made or purchased and mutually selected. Naturally your wedding date could be inscribed.

In biblical literature cups are used in richly symbolic ways. For Christians the most significant refer-

---

*This is based on an idea in Jack Lundin's book *Celebrations for Special Days and Occasions* (Harper & Row, 1971). I am interested in having your suggestions on other ways in which wedding anniversaries may be celebrated. Please direct these to me % Abingdon Press, 201 Eighth Avenue, South, Nashville, Tennessee 37202.

ence to the cup is found in connection with its use in the Eucharist. As the disciples at the Lord's Supper drank from the cup, described by our Lord as representing his atonement for our sins, they became profoundly involved in receiving heaven's gift. Thus the cup symbolizes the believer's participation in experiences that can be celebrated with reverence. Used in connection with your marriage anniversary, the cup can symbolize the sense of shared destiny, of divine provision, of a future bright with hope.

With thoughts such as these in mind, you can drink from your cup and derive meaning that takes on the dimension added by enlightened imagination. For this is the power of the symbol—to go beyond the form to the essence, to go beyond the material to the spiritual. And as you sound the depths of this shared moment, you may become aware of the presence of him who long ago "took the cup, and gave thanks, and gave it to them, saying, Drink ye all of it."

A Service to Celebrate
A Silver or Golden Wedding
Anniversary

While wedding anniversaries are largely social occasions, some couples desire a religious service to commemorate the event. The following service was created for a golden wedding but is equally useful for the silver anniversary.

The minister

Dearly beloved, we are gathered here in the sight of God and in the presence of this company to help this couple renew the sacred vows which they took *fifty* years ago on this day. This *half* century of happy married life has ripened into a love and loyalty and a devotion that has become a blessing and a benediction to all who know them.

After *fifty* years of happy married life they stand in our presence to bear witness to the fact that marriage is an honorable estate; that it is instituted of God; that it does signify the mystical union between Christ and his Church; that Christ does make married life and home life happy and beautiful and sacred, even as he brought joy and beauty and sacredness into the marriage at Cana of Galilee, which he blessed with his presence.

These loved ones are ready to give testimony to the fact that marriage is an honorable thing among all men, and therefore is not to be entered into unadvisedly or lightly, but reverently, discreetly, soberly, and in the spirit of, in the presence of, and in the fear of God. In this holy estate these two persons have lived for *fifty* years, and they come now to renew their covenant, their love, their loyalty, their devotion to each other. In the presence of Christ, who has led them in the midst of joy and difficulty, they give to each other their heart and their hand, all that they have and all that they are.

To the man

N————, *fifty* years ago you pledged your troth to N————, and you took her to be your wedded wife, to live with her after God's ordinance in the holy estate of matrimony. At that time you promised to love her, honor her, and cherish her. You also promised to be loyal to her whether rich or poor, in sickness or in health. These *fifty* years have found you to be faithful to this pledge. Will you, therefore, now at the close of this *half* century, in the presence of God, *in the presence of your children, in the presence of your grandchildren,* and in the presence of these friends that have gathered here, renew these vows, and continue this devotion to her so long as you both shall live?

Answer

I will.

To the woman

N———, *fifty* years ago you pledged your troth to N———, and you took him to be your wedded husband, to live with him after God's ordinance in the holy estate of matrimony. At that time you promised to love him, honor him, and cherish him. You also promised to be loyal to him whether rich or poor, in sickness or in health. These *fifty* years have likewise found you to be faithful to this pledge. Will you, therefore, also, now at the close of this *half* century, in the presence of God, *in the presence of your children, in the presence of your grandchildren*, and in the presence of these friends that have gathered here, renew these vows, and continue this devotion to him so long as you both shall live?

Answer

I will.

The minister

What evidence do you have of this your renewed vow?

Then they may give each other rings, or the man may present a ring to the woman, repeating after the minister:

With this ring I renew my vow of love and loyalty. I continue to endow you with my heart's affection and my worldly goods. In the name of God the Father, the Son, and the Holy Spirit. Amen.

Then they join right hands as the minister says:

Forasmuch as *N*——— and *N*——— have renewed their covenant, and have witnessed the same before God and in the presence of this company, and have given their pledge each to the other, and have declared the same by the giving and the receiving of *a ring,* and by the joining of their hands, I pray God's blessings and benediction upon them.

Prayer

Almighty God our heavenly Father, who did institute the holy estate of matrimony for the mutual help and comfort of your children; we thank you that you have preserved these your servants through *fifty* years of married life. We praise you for your goodness to them in making their union one of love, peace, and happiness; and that through your grace they have been able to keep their vow and covenant. Protect and prosper them, we beseech you, through the years to come. Multiply your blessings upon them. May they abound in love and bear together willingly the burdens of life. Encourage and sustain them in all godly living; and may their home continue to be a place of prayer, consecration, and joy. Let your benediction rest upon them to their life's end, and finally give them a joyful entrance into your blessed kingdom; through Jesus Christ our Lord. *Amen.*

Benediction

The Lord bless you and keep you; the Lord make his face shine upon you, and be gracious unto you; the Lord lift up his countenance upon you, and give you peace, now and evermore. *Amen.*